WHILE STARING AT THE STARS

CONTEMPLATING THE UNIVERSE FROM MY ROOFTOP

PRAKRITI PANDEY

Made with ♥ on the Notion Press Platform
www.notionpress.com

This book is a love letter to my younger self, the dreamer who pondered the mysteries of teenage minds beneath the twinkling sky. Those magical nights of curiosity and creativity breathe life into every single word within these pages.

Contents

FOREWORD

Welcome to"*While Staring at the Stars*"!

This book is like a cozy blanket on a chilly night, inviting you to snuggle up and take a journey through the wonders of the universe and the depths of our hearts.

Here, you'll find stories and thoughts that explore the beauty of the night sky and the feelings that stir inside us when we gaze at the stars. It's a bit like having few grandma lessons where each twinkle above holds a secret

Through these pages, we'll talk about spirituality, love, music ,kindness and how we see the world around us. It's like having a heart-to-heart conversation with a dear friend, where we share our thoughts and dreams while sipping on a warm cup of tea.

So, as you flip through this book, let it be a gentle reminder to pause, to ponder, and to find joy in the simple things. Because sometimes, amidst the hustle and bustle of life, all we need is a moment to look up at the stars and remember the magic that surrounds us.

With warm wishes,

Prakriti Pandey

PREFACE

In the tranquil hills of Uttarakhand, amidst the whispering winds and rustling leaves, I found solace and inspiration under the vast expanse of the night sky. From the tender age of childhood to the precipice of young adulthood, my journey has been intertwined with the timeless allure of the cosmos.

This book, "While Staring at the Stars," is a collection of reflections, musings, and memories inspired by my lifelong fascination with the stars. It is a tribute to the countless nights spent gazing upward, lost in the beauty and wonder of the universe.

Through these pages, I invite you to join me on a journey of introspection and discovery. From the simple joys of stargazing with my grandparents in Naukuchiya Tal to the profound moments of contemplation under the twinkling night sky, each chapter is a glimpse into the depths of my imagination and the mysteries of the cosmos.

As you turn the pages, may you find yourself transported to the tranquil hills of Uttarakhand, where the stars shine brightly and dreams take flight. May you be inspired to embrace the magic of the unknown and embark on your own journey of exploration and self-discovery.

Thank you for joining me on this celestial voyage. Together, let us explore the wonders of the universe, one star at a time.

Acknowledgements

I would like to express my heartfelt gratitude to the universe for the endless inspiration it has bestowed upon me, fueling my passion for stargazing and storytelling.

To my beloved grandparents, Nanaji and Nani, your love and wisdom have been the guiding stars of my life's journey. Thank you for nurturing my curiosity about the cosmos and for instilling in me a deep appreciation for the wonders of the universe.

To my family, friends, and mentors, your unwavering support and encouragement have been my source of strength. Your belief in me has propelled me forward, even in the face of uncertainty.

To the stars themselves, for their timeless beauty and boundless wisdom. You have been my constant companions, filling my heart with wonder and awe with each twinkle in the night sky.

And lastly, to the readers, thank you for joining me on this celestial adventure. May the pages of this book spark your curiosity and inspire you to embrace the magic of the unknown.

With deepest gratitude,
Prakriti Pandey

Prologue

In the quiet hills of Uttarakhand, where the air is crisp and the nights are alive with the whispering winds, there lies a world of magic and mystery waiting to be discovered. It is a world where time seems to stand still, and the stars above tell stories that have been whispered through the ages.

It is here, amidst the tranquil beauty of nature's embrace, that our journey begins. In the pages that follow, we will embark on an adventure of the mind and spirit, guided by the twinkling lights of the night sky.

But before we delve into the depths of the cosmos and the wonders it holds, let us take a moment to pause and reflect on the journey that has brought us here. For it is in the quiet moments of contemplation and reflection that we find the true meaning of our existence, and the answers to the questions that lie deep within our souls.

So let us cast our gaze upward, toward the stars that have illuminated the path of countless dreamers before us. And as we journey into the unknown, may we find inspiration, wonder, and a sense of awe in the boundless expanse of the universe.

I

INTRODUCTION

Living in Uttarakhand's hills, with the serenity of Naukuchiya Tal, I enjoyed my days with pleasure in the peaceful world that surrounded me as a child. It was another affair, day after day, to start each adventure with Nanaji and Nani, and then add Chota Mama to our team. From the comfort of a roof covered with a chatai mat and built over our modest dwelling, I discovered my retreat. During the day, I used to sit there, enjoying the sun on my face and staring out into the vast blue sky above me. Since I was a child, I have been mesmerized by words and the ability to weave stories out of them. As a 17-year-old girl with dreams and an insatiable curiosity, I have always yearned for an outlet to express my thoughts and experiences.

And oh, the nights! As darkness enveloped the world, a breathtaking spectacle unfolded above me. I would lay on my back, the chatai beneath me, and lose myself in the mesmerizing dance of the twinkling stars. In those moments, with the universe stretched out before me, I couldn't help but wonder - would I ever touch those stars?

Could I one day become an astronaut, exploring the mysteries of space?

Growing up, I found solace in the pages of books, escaping into fantastical worlds and exploring the depths of my imagination. But as much as I loved getting lost in the stories of others, I knew deep down that I had stories of my own to tell.

I wanted to create something raw and authentic, a window into the kaleidoscope of my mind. I wanted to pour my heart onto the pages, weaving together tales of adventure, moments of self-discovery, and glimpses of the world through my eyes.

> "*Writing this book isn't just about fulfilling a childhood dream; it's about embracing my voice and owning my story. It's about stepping out of my comfort zone and daring to be vulnerable. And so, the idea of writing a book became a cherished dream of mine, a beacon of light guiding me through the ups and downs of adolescence. I made a promise to myself that* ***I would write a book before I turned 20****, a book that would be a reflection of my inner most thoughts and experience while i was a kid.*"

I remember being 13 years old, lying on the *takht*, staring up at the twinkling stars scattered across the night sky. As I gazed at those distant lights, a question began to form in my mind: could I ever write a book?

It seemed like such a daunting idea at the time. I was just a kid with big dreams and an even bigger imagination. The thought of putting pen to paper and crafting a story that would captivate readers felt like an impossible task.

But as I lay there beneath the vast expanse of the universe, something inside me stirred. It was a spark of curiosity and determination, a flicker of hope that whispered, "Why not?"

In that moment, surrounded by the quiet beauty of the night, I made a silent vow to myself. I would explore the depths of my imagination, weaving together characters and worlds that lived only in my mind. I would pour my heart and soul into every word, letting my creativity flow freely like a river carving its path through the landscape.

As the years passed, that dream never left me. It lingered in the back of my mind, a constant reminder of the promise I had made to myself on that starry night. And though there were moments of doubt and uncertainty, I refused to give up on my aspirations.

Now, as I look back on that 13-year-old dreamer staring up at the stars, I realize that writing a book was never just a possibility – it was destiny. It was the journey I was meant to embark on, the story waiting to be told.

And so, with each word I write, I honor that young dreamer and the dreams that continue to guide me forward. For I know now that anything is possible, even reaching for the stars and turning them into stories.

So, here I am, embarking on this journey of self-expression and creativity, armed with nothing but my pen and my imagination. This book is my love letter to the teenage girl who believed in possibilities

And as I set out to write these pages, I invite you to join me on this adventure, to laugh, to cry, and to dream alongside me. Because in the end, isn't that what storytelling is all about? Connecting hearts, inspiring minds, and sharing the beauty of being human.

"In "While Staring at the Stars," I invite you to join me on a journey through the memories and musings of a child who dared to dream amidst the hills of Uttarakhand. Together, let us rediscover the magic of staring at the stars, and the endless potential that lies within each of us, waiting to be explored."

Thank you for being a part of this journey. Let's write our stories together

With love and endless possibilities

II

THE NIGHT SKY

Nani's house, nestled amidst the tranquil hills of Uttarakhand, was more than just a home; it was a place where the wonders of the night sky unfolded before my very eyes. As the sun dipped below the horizon and darkness descended upon the world, a new realm of beauty and wonder revealed itself above.

The stars, like tiny diamonds scattered across an endless expanse of velvet, adorned the night sky in a breathtaking display of celestial splendor. From the brightest constellations to the faintest specks of light, each star held its own unique allure, beckoning me to gaze upward in awe and reverence.

On Nani's rooftop, with the gentle night breeze and the faraway sound of crickets, I felt peaceful under the starry sky. Looking up at the stars made me feel calm and relaxed, like a gentle wave washing away my worries. It was like time stopped, and all the busy things in life didn't matter. I felt connected to everything – the universe, nature, and all the people who had been on that rooftop before me.

Nani's house was like a safe place under the stars, where I could forget about everything else and just enjoy the beauty of the night sky. Sitting on that simple mat on the rooftop, I learned to appreciate the little things in life and how amazing the stars are. It was a special place where I could feel happy and content, surrounded by the magic of the night sky.

Growing up, I was incredibly lucky to have parents who believed in me. They didn't just let me dream, they encouraged me to dream big. They never told me what I couldn't do, and they always believed in me, no matter what. Because of them, I always knew I could do anything I wanted. I could be anything I wanted. They taught me to believe in myself and to never give up on my dreams. With their support, I dared to dream big. I saw myself as a pioneer, someone who would break new ground and make a difference in the world. They taught me that the possibilities were endless, and that I could go as far as my dreams would take me.

As a young adventurer of 11, gazing up at the star-studded expanse above, I couldn't resist being filled with awe and a burning desire to explore the unknown that lay ahead.

Every twinkling star felt like a promise, a glimpse into the limitless possibilities that awaited me on life's path. My mind raced with thoughts of the challenges I would inevitably encounter and how I would muster the courage and determination to overcome them. The future stretched out before me like an uncharted ocean, both intimidating and exhilarating in its endlessness. However, alongside the uncertainty, a surge of excitement and anticipation coursed through me. The night sky seemed to whisper tantalizing tales of adventures to be had, dreams to be realized, and moments of pure bliss.

As I stood beneath the celestial canopy, my imagination soared, weaving intricate tales of adventure and triumph. I envisioned myself as a fearless explorer charting uncharted territories, a daring astronaut venturing into the unknown depths of space, and a wise sage unraveling the secrets of the universe.

But amidst these flights of fancy, a nagging sense of uncertainty lingered, whispering doubts and fears into the recesses of my mind. What if I stumbled and fell? What if my dreams remained forever out of reach? What if the future held challenges too daunting to overcome?

It was during these moments of introspection that my Nani's gentle voice would echo in my ears, her words a beacon of wisdom and reassurance. "Child," she would say, her voice soft yet resolute, "the stars above may seem distant and unreachable, but they are not beyond your grasp. Each one holds a story of resilience and perseverance, a testament to the human spirit's boundless capacity for growth and transformation."

Her words were like a soothing balm to my restless soul, offering comfort and guidance in times of uncertainty. She taught me to embrace the unknown with a sense of curiosity and wonder, to view challenges as opportunities for growth rather than obstacles to be feared.

And so, as I stood beneath the night sky, bathed in the ethereal glow of a million stars, I made a silent vow to heed my Nani's words and face the future with courage and determination. For in the depths of the unknown, amidst the swirling chaos of life, lay the promise of adventure, discovery, and endless possibility.

As I sat on a weathered wooden plank (तख्त) under the vast expanse of the night sky, surrounded by the soft whispers of the breeze and the rhythmic symphony of nature, I found myself enveloped in a moment of profound solitude. In that tranquil space, devoid of distractions, my thoughts turned to the celestial wonders that adorned the heavens above.

Finding Clarity Amidst the Darkness

> *"As I gazed upward, my gaze drawn to the luminous orb of the moon, I found solace in its serene presence. It was a reminder that even in the darkest of nights, there exists a beacon of light to guide us through the shadows, illuminating the path ahead with its gentle glow."*

Living in the hills of Uttarakhand and witnessing the night sky every day sounds truly magical and dreamlike indeed. The pristine beauty of the mountains combined with the clear, unpolluted skies provides an ideal environment for star gazing. The feeling of being surrounded by nature and gazing up at the vast expanse of the night sky filled with twinkling stars can be an incredibly enriching and soulful experience.

If you feel a deep love for star gazing and a strong connection to the wonders of the cosmos, then it's possible that you have a passion for astronomy. Many people find solace, inspiration, and a sense of wonder in exploring the mysteries of the universe through observing the stars and celestial objects.

Living in such a breathtaking environment as the hills of Uttarakhand would provide you with ample opportunities to indulge in your passion for star gazing. Whether it's identifying constellations, observing planets, or simply marveling at the beauty of the Milky Way stretching across the night sky, each night would offer a new adventure and a chance to deepen your appreciation for the cosmos.

Remember, pursuing your passion for star gazing can be a fulfilling journey that not only enriches your own life but also inspires others to look up and wonder about the universe around us. So, embrace your love for the stars and continue to let the magic of the night sky ignite your curiosity and imagination.

III

CHAPTER OF SPIRITUALITY

The concept of spirituality for me begin with Nani by my side, I discovered the magic of devotion and the warmth of prayer. Each morning, as the sun tiptoed above the horizon, painting the sky in hues of amber and rose, we'd nestle together in silent reverence, offering our hopes and gratitude to the universe. Through her patient guidance, I learned to find peace in moments of quiet, to seek solace in the whispers of the breeze, and to delight in the sheer miracle of existence.

> *"If there's a God out there, I often wonder what I'd ask myself when tough times hit. It's funny how those hard times push me to be kinder every time. Every time I'm hurt, I feel closer to God."*

Life's been tough, but it's taught me something important: when things get rough, turning to God brings peace. It's like God's there, guiding me to be kind and understanding, especially when life gets hard.

When life throws its curveballs, I find comfort in God, seeking solace deep within. These experiences have taught me to be kind, not just to others but also to myself.

> *"Every time I've been hurt, it made me realize how important kindness is. I've learned to show compassion to those hurting, lend an ear to those in need, and forgive to heal."*

In God's embrace, I've found the courage to face life's challenges with kindness and humility. And through it all, I've come to understand that kindness isn't just nice – it is what connects us to God and each other.

> *"So, if I had to ask something of myself in front of God, it would be simple: always choose kindness, even when things are tough. Because it's through kindness that we truly connect with God and show our humanity."*

As we delved into the rituals of our faith, I found myself drawn deeper into the spiritual tapestry of life. The ancient chants we shared became melodies that danced through my soul, and the flickering flame of our household diya became a beacon of warmth that illuminated my path.

Yet, beyond the rituals and ceremonies, it was Nani's unshakeable faith and boundless love that truly captivated me. In her everyday gestures and loving gaze, I witnessed the embodiment of spirituality – a gentle strength that forwarded from a heart overflowing with kindness and compassion.

So, with each passing day, I took my small steps along the spiritual journey, guided by Nani's wisdom and the love she so generously shared. In her comforting presence, I discovered that true spirituality isn't about grand gestures or elaborate rituals; it's about the simple act of opening our hearts to love and empathy.

In the sanctuary of Nani's love, I found my first glimpses of the divine, and it was there that I began my tender journey towards becoming the spiritual being I am today.

My Nani always emphasized that spirituality transcends mere rituals or chanting the names of gods. For her, it was about embodying empathy and selflessness in our daily lives. She taught me that true spirituality lies in how we treat others, in the kindness and compassion we show to those around us. Through her words and actions, she demonstrated the importance of empathy, of understanding and sharing in the experiences of others. Nani believed that being spiritually connected meant reaching out a helping hand to those in need, without expecting anything in return. It was about nurturing a genuine concern for the well-being of others and striving to make a positive difference in the world. In essence, she taught me that the essence of spirituality lies in our capacity to love, to empathize, and to serve others with an open heart and a generous spirit.

"*Wisdom in Childhood Myths*"

Even though I'm still young, I'll admit that I take Nani's little myths pretty seriously – and maybe that's okay! Growing up, Nani's stories were more than just tales; they were lessons in disguise, sprinkled with a bit of magic and a whole lot of love.

Sure, some might call them *"choti moti"* myths, but to me, they're treasures of wisdom passed down through generations. From the mischievous antics of ancient deities to the moral lessons hidden in folktales, each story holds a nugget of truth waiting to be discovered.

As I navigate the ups and downs of life, I find myself turning to these childhood myths for guidance and reassurance. There's something comforting about the familiar rhythms of these stories, something reassuring in the way they remind me that I'm not alone in this journey.

So, while others might scoff at Nani's tales as mere superstitions, I'll continue to cherish them as the precious gems they are. After all, who's to say that a little bit of magic and a whole lot of love can't hold the key to unlocking life's mysteries?

As a child, I always believed that growing up would bring nothing but good things. It seemed like such a simple and straightforward concept: become an adult, and everything would fall into place. Life would be smooth sailing, filled with happiness and success. But as I journeyed through the years and stepped into adulthood, reality hit me hard. Life unfolded in ways I never could have imagined, and I found myself facing a series of unexpected challenges and experiences.

One of the first things I realized as I grew older was that life is unpredictable. No matter how much we plan or hope for a certain outcome, there are always unforeseen twists and turns that can throw us off course. It's like walking down a winding road, never quite knowing what lies around the next bend. As a child, I never understood this aspect of life. I thought everything was black and white, but now I see that there are endless shades of gray.

Another lesson that life taught me was that it's not always fair. As a child, I had a simplistic view of justice – good things happen to good people, and bad things happen to bad people. But as I grew older, I witnessed firsthand the injustices and inequalities that exist in the world. I saw hardworking individuals struggle to make ends meet while others seemed to effortlessly climb the ladder of success. I learned that life doesn't always play by the rules, and sometimes, it's the most undeserving who come out on top.

Perhaps the most profound realization I had as I navigated through adulthood was the fragility of life itself. As a child, I felt invincible, as if nothing could touch me. But as I grew older, I began to understand just how fragile and fleeting life can be. I experienced loss and heartache, watching loved ones pass away and dreams slip through my fingers. I learned that life is precious and should never be taken for granted, for tomorrow is never guaranteed.

Despite the many challenges and hardships I faced as I grew older, I also discovered moments of immense beauty and joy. I found love in unexpected places, forged meaningful connections with others, and pursued passions that filled my soul with purpose. I learned to appreciate the simple pleasures in life – a warm hug from a friend, a breathtaking sunset, the laughter of children playing in the park.

Through it all, I came to understand that growing up is not just about getting older; it's about growing wiser and more resilient. It's about embracing the complexities of life and finding strength in the face of adversity. It's about holding onto hope and never losing sight of the beauty that surrounds us, even in the darkest of times.

So, while life may not have turned out exactly as I expected, I wouldn't change a thing. Every twist and turn, every joy and sorrow, has shaped me into the person I am today. And for that, I am grateful.

> *"As a teenager, I find myself still exploring the depths of spirituality, yet I am anchored by the profound teachings instilled in me by my nani. Though my understanding may be limited at this stage of my life; I hold steadfast to the wisdom she has imparted, cherishing it as a beacon of guidance. With each lesson she shared, I embraced it wholeheartedly, knowing that her words carried the weight of experience and love."*

While I may not possess an extensive knowledge of spirituality, my commitment to honoring my nani's teachings remains unwavering. Her words echo in my heart, guiding me along a path of self-discovery and enlightenment. As I continue to journey through life, I am determined to uphold the values she instilled in me, knowing that they serve as a compass for navigating the complexities of the world.

In the face of uncertainty and the vastness of spiritual exploration, I take solace in the teachings of my nani, knowing that her wisdom will continue to illuminate my path. With humility and gratitude, I embrace the opportunity to learn and grow, carrying forward the legacy of love and enlightenment she has entrusted to me.

When I was young, I used to talk a lot of nonsense with my friends without realizing how it could affect our friendships. Looking back, I can see that I wasn't being true to myself or to them. Over time, I lost many of those friendships because I wasn't being genuine.

As I got older, I started to understand the importance of being true to myself and to others. I realized that having real connections with people is more important than just talking about random stuff. It took losing those friendships for me to realize this, but I'm grateful for the lesson.

One thing I used to find really boring was worshiping or doing spiritual activities. I didn't see the point in it, and I didn't understand why people did it. But as I grew older, I started to see things differently. I began to feel a deeper connection to these practices and to understand their significance.

Now, I realize how important it is to be true to myself and to honor my beliefs and values. I've learned that being genuine in my relationships and in everything I do is essential for building strong connections and finding happiness. And even though I lost some friendships along the way, I'm grateful for the lessons I've learned and for the person I've become.

Now it feels like there's a gap between me and my friends who are the same age as me is kinda confusing. It's like we're not on the same page, even though we're all from the same time. When I talk to them, it feels like we're speaking different languages. We have things in common, but our views and what's important to us seem different.

Maybe it's because things are changing so fast, like new technology and how society sees things. Some of my friends are really into all the latest stuff and spending a lot of time online, but I'm more into having real talks and deeper connections. It's like we're living in different worlds sometimes.

I sometimes feel like I'm on the outside looking in, watching everyone else having fun and talking about things that don't really interest me. It's not that I don't care, but I want more than just chatting about random stuff or what's popular right now.

Even though it's hard sometimes, I believe there are people out there who feel the same way I do. Maybe I just haven't found them yet. For now, I'll keep trying to connect with others and hope to find friends who get where I'm coming from.

IV

HOME IS A PERSON

I've always believed that home is not just a building or location, but a place where you feel at peace with someone who loves you. That special person creates a sense of comfort and safety, where you can relax and let go of your worries and responsibilities. For me, home has always been my grandmother, *Nani*. With her, I could be my true self, making silly jokes and playing around without feeling judged. She had a gift for bringing out my inner child and reminding me of the joy of being carefree and curious.

> *"and in case a place like home exists it would surely be "nani ka ghar " for me , no wonder why."*

Nani's nurturing love extended beyond just her creations; it was woven into every aspect of my upbringing, even in the most unexpected gestures like ensuring I drank the milk from her cow or adding extra ghee to my *roti or dal.*

Despite my initial reluctance, Nani's insistence on drinking the milk from her cow became a cherished ritual. With a twinkle in her eye and a warm smile, she would lovingly prepare a glass of milk, emphasizing its nutritional benefits and the care with which it was sourced. And though I may have hesitated at first, I soon came to appreciate the wholesome goodness and the comforting reassurance that came with each sip.

Similarly, Nani's habit of generously adding extra ghee to my roti or dal became a symbol of her love and affection. With each bite, I could taste the richness and warmth of her care, a tangible reminder of her desire to ensure my well-being and happiness.

In these seemingly small acts of kindness, I found a profound expression of Nani's love and devotion. It was her way of nurturing not just my body, but also my spirit, ensuring that I felt loved, cherished, and cared for in every moment of my life.

Looking back, I am grateful for Nani's unwavering love and the countless ways in which she showered me with affection. From her homemade delicacies to her heartfelt gestures, her love continues to nourish me, body and soul, filling my heart with warmth and gratitude for the precious memories we shared.

Whether it was spending hours stargazing on the rooftop, telling stories by the crackling fire, or simply sharing moments of quiet companionship, Nani's presence enveloped me like a cozy blanket, offering solace and reassurance in a world full of uncertainties.

In her company, I found the freedom to express myself without fear of judgment or criticism. I reveled in the simple pleasures of life, basking in the pure, unadulterated joy of being fully present in the moment.

Through her nurturing love and unwavering support, Nani became the embodiment of home – a refuge where my heart felt safe, my soul felt nourished, and my spirit felt free to soar. In her presence, I discovered that home isn't just a place we return to at the end of the day, but a person who holds us in their heart and makes us feel truly alive.

Nani's *aalu tamatar ki sabji* holds a special place in my heart, not just for its delicious taste, but for the memories it evokes of cozy evenings spent in her kitchen, surrounded by the comforting aromas of home-cooked meals and the laughter of loved ones.

The simplicity of this dish belies its rich flavors and comforting warmth. Fresh tomatoes simmered with tender chunks of potatoes in a fragrant blend of spices, infused with the rich aroma of Nani's homemade *ghee* – it's a dish that speaks of love, tradition, and the simple joys of home.

Each bite is a journey back to my childhood, a taste of nostalgia that transports me to simpler times and cherished memories. Whether enjoyed with fluffy rotis fresh from the stove or steaming bowls of fragrant rice, Nani's aalu tamatar ki sabji is a culinary masterpiece that never fails to bring a smile to my face and warmth to my soul.

But beyond its delectable taste, this dish is a testament to the love and care that Nani pours into everything she does. It's a labor of love, crafted with her own hands and seasoned with the warmth of her heart. And with each bite, I am reminded of the countless meals she has prepared with love, nourishing both body and soul with her culinary creations.

In Nani's kitchen, every dish tells a story – a story of love, tradition, and the timeless bond between generations. And as I savor each spoonful of her aalu tamatar ki sabji, I am reminded that home is not just a place, but a feeling – a feeling of love, warmth, and belonging that Nani's cooking never fails to evoke.

Just as stars light up the night, this person fills our lives with laughter, comfort, and the kind of joy that makes us feel like kids again. With them, we can let our guard down, act silly, and embrace the simple pleasures of life without fear of judgment.

They're our rock, our constant, our North Star in the vastness of space. Their love and support light up our darkest moments, reminding us that no matter how far we roam, we'll always find our way back home—to the person who makes our universe feel a little less lonely and a lot more like home.

Love Beyond Borders: Lessons from Nani's Unwavering Devotion

I learned that love is everlasting when my Nani's mother passed away. My Nani adored her mother so deeply that she took on the rituals typically performed by her brothers. Despite being the only girl among four brothers, even after her marriage and moving to a different house, she continued these traditions.

Even today, when she prepares evening tea, she brings a cup filled with water and places it near a flowering plant. This simple act hits me hard every day.

Through Nani's devotion, I've come to understand that love knows no boundaries. It transcends time and space, remaining steadfast even after loved ones have passed on. Nani's actions remind me that true love is not bound by circumstances or distance; it is a force that continues to nourish and sustain us, even in the face of loss and change.

Her gesture of placing water near the plant symbolizes her eternal connection with her mother, a bond that remains unbroken despite the passage of time. It serves as a poignant reminder that love, like life itself, is immortal.

O*h, how I miss those rainy days from my childhood when school was canceled. It was like a special gift from the sky! My nani would prepare a simple lunch for us, and we'd all huddle together under cozy blankets while we ate. The raindrops tapping on the windowpane created a soothing rhythm that added to the warmth of our little indoor picnic.*

Wrapped snugly in our razai, we savored the homemade treats Nani had lovingly packed for us – sandwiches filled with delicious fillings, crunchy chips, and sweet treats that always made us smile. It was comfort food at its finest, made even more special by the love and care that Nani poured into every bite.

As we sat together on the couch, plates balanced on our laps, we would flip through the channels until we found our favorite cartoons: "Oswald" and "Phineas and Ferb." Those animated worlds became our escape, filling our hearts with joy and laughter as we watched the colorful characters embark on their adventures.

The sound of our laughter mingled with the gentle patter of rain outside, creating a symphony of happiness that echoed through the room. In those moments, surrounded by the love of my nani and the magic of childhood, all my worries melted away, replaced by a sense of pure contentment.

Now, as I look back on those rainy days of my youth, a wave of nostalgia washes over me. I find myself yearning to relive those carefree moments, to feel the warmth of my nani's love enveloping me like a cozy blanket once again. The memories of those simple joys bring a smile to my face, reminding me of the beauty and innocence of childhood.

Though those days may be gone, their memory remains etched in my heart as a cherished treasure. And on rainy days like today, as I listen to the soft patter of rain outside my window, I can't help but feel grateful for the precious moments I shared with my nani.

stars and home

Sitting beneath the stars feels like home to me. It's a simple pleasure that brings me immense joy and comfort. Whenever I gaze up at the night sky, I feel a sense of belonging and connection to something greater than myself.

There's something magical about the stars twinkling above, like they're whispering secrets to me from the heavens. Each star seems to hold a story, a reminder of the vastness and beauty of the universe. And as I sit there, surrounded by the stillness of the night, I can't help but feel a sense of peace wash over me.

In those moments beneath the stars, everything else fades away. Worries and stresses melt into the background, replaced by a feeling of serenity and calm. It's like the weight of the world is lifted off my shoulders, and I'm free to simply be.

Sometimes, I'll sit beneath the stars with friends or loved ones, sharing stories and laughter as we marvel at the beauty above. Other times, I'll sit alone, lost in my own thoughts and reflections. But no matter who I'm with or what I'm doing, being beneath the stars always feels like coming home.

I think part of the reason why sitting beneath the stars feels so comforting to me is because it's a reminder of my place in the universe. In the grand scheme of things, my problems and worries seem small and insignificant. It's humbling to realize that I'm just one small speck in a vast cosmos, and yet, I'm a part of something infinitely greater.

There's also a sense of wonder and awe that comes with stargazing. Each time I look up at the sky, I'm reminded of the mysteries that lie beyond our planet. I think about the countless stars and galaxies stretching out into infinity, and I'm filled with a sense of wonder at the sheer magnitude of it all.

But amidst the vastness of space, there's also a feeling of closeness and intimacy. The stars may be millions of miles away, but they still feel like old friends, keeping watch over me as I sit below. It's a comforting thought, knowing that no matter where I go or what I do, the stars will always be there, shining down on me.

In a world that often feels chaotic and uncertain, sitting beneath the stars is a reminder of the constants in life. It's a reminder that no matter what happens, there's beauty and wonder to be found in the world around us. And for me, that's what makes sitting beneath the stars feel like home.

V

KINDNESS APPROVES A LOT

Being kind is really good and makes a big difference. When I say "kindness approves a lot," it means that being nice is seen as a really good thing and people like it a lot. It shows that being kind is not just a nice thing to do, but it's also something that has a big positive impact on others and situations. In simple terms, it means that being kind is something that everyone thinks is great and makes a big difference in making things better.

> "*While browsing through social media, I stumbled upon a thought-provoking statement: "If God doesn't give you instant results when you're kind to someone, it's the same God who doesn't punish you instantly for your sins." This message struck a chord within me, prompting me to reflect on the nature of kindness and divine justice.*"

In a world where instant gratification often reigns supreme, the concept of delayed rewards for acts of kindness challenges our expectations. We live in a society that thrives on immediate outcomes, where the value of our actions is often measured by the instant feedback we receive. However, the notion that kindness may not always yield instant results challenges this paradigm, reminding us of the importance of patience and perseverance in our pursuit of goodness.

Similarly, the idea that divine punishment for wrongdoing may not be meted out immediately challenges our understanding of justice. In a world where we often seek swift retribution for wrongdoing, the concept of divine patience and mercy offers a profound reminder of the boundless compassion of a higher power. It encourages us to view our actions through the lens of forgiveness and redemption, recognizing that even in our moments of weakness, there is always the opportunity for growth and transformation.

Ultimately, the message encapsulated in this statement serves as a powerful reminder of the complex interplay between kindness, justice, and divine providence. It challenges us to reevaluate our expectations and assumptions, urging us to embrace the virtues of patience, compassion, and faith as we navigate the complexities of life's journey.

> *"In the gentle cadence of her voice, my nani imparted a timeless lesson that has stayed with me through the years. "Thik hai unko shi laga hamare sath galat karke, lekin agar ham bhi unke jaise ho jayenge to farak kya rahega?" These words, spoken in Hindi, hold a wisdom that transcends language*

and time."

In essence, my nani's message was simple yet profound: even when others wrong us, it is essential to uphold our principles and act with integrity. By responding with kindness and grace, we elevate ourselves above the hurt and negativity, refusing to be dragged down to the same level as those who have wronged us.

This lesson resonates deeply with me, reminding me of the importance of maintaining my moral compass even in the face of adversity. It teaches me that true strength lies not in seeking revenge or succumbing to bitterness, but in choosing forgiveness and compassion.

My nani's words serve as a guiding light, illuminating the path of righteousness even in the darkest of times. They remind me that our actions define who we are, and by choosing to do right by others, we cultivate a spirit of goodness and grace that transcends the challenges we may face.

As an author, I am grateful for the wisdom passed down to me by my nani. Her teachings continue to inspire and guide me, shaping not only my writing but also my approach to life. Through her words, I am reminded of the profound impact that kindness and integrity can have, both in our personal relationships and in the broader tapestry of humanity.

Nani's teachings about kindness and the universe's response to our actions were simple yet profound. She often emphasized the importance of treating others with kindness and respect, regardless of how they treated us in return. According to Nani, the universe operates on the principle of karma – the idea that our actions, both good and bad, have consequences that come back to us in some way.

Nani's lessons about karma were not about seeking instant rewards for our good deeds, but rather about understanding that our actions have a ripple effect that can impact our lives in the long run. She would often say, "The universe notices when we do good things, and it has a way of giving back to us in its own time."

For Nani, kindness was not just a virtue, but a way of life. She believed that by spreading kindness and positivity, we could create a brighter and more harmonious world for ourselves and others. Her teachings emphasized the importance of being mindful of our actions and the energy we put out into the world, knowing that it would eventually come back to us in some form.

As a child, I was inspired by Nani's words and the way she lived her life with compassion and empathy. Her teachings about kindness and karma shaped my understanding of the world and influenced the way I interacted with others. I learned to be more mindful of my actions and to always strive to treat others with kindness, knowing that it would ultimately come back to me in positive ways.

Through Nani's guidance, I came to understand that kindness is not just a fleeting gesture, but a powerful force that has the ability to shape our lives and the world around us. Her lessons about karma taught me to be patient and trust in the universe's ability to reward acts of kindness in its own time. And most importantly, her example showed me that by living a life filled with kindness and compassion, we can create a more beautiful and fulfilling existence for ourselves and those around us.

Feeling really happy and excited like a child can be a way of connecting with something deeper inside us, which some people call spirituality. It's like when we're so excited about something that we forget about everything else and just enjoy the moment. This childlike excitement helps us appreciate the little things in life and feel connected to the world around us. It's all about feeling joyful, curious, and amazed by the world, just like a kid does. And when we feel this way, it can make us feel more alive and connected to something bigger than ourselves.

One problem that some people in Generation Z (Gen Z) face is being unkind, and technology like smartphones and social media can sometimes make this worse. Gen Z grew up with smartphones and the internet, which can be good for staying connected, but it also means they spend a lot of time online.

On social media, people often show only the best parts of their lives, which can make others feel bad about themselves. This can lead to people being mean or not caring about others' feelings. Also, online, it's easier to say hurtful things because you're not talking face-to-face with someone.

Sometimes, because everything moves so quickly online, people forget to take the time to really understand each other's feelings. They might not think about how their words or actions affect others.

To fix this, it's important for Gen Z to be mindful of how they act online. They should think about how their words and actions might make others feel. Learning to be kind online, just like in person, is important for building good relationships and making the internet a nicer place for everyone.

It's true that in Generation Z, there's a trend of hurting people that might not have been as common in the past, like in the 90s. With the rise of social media and online communication, some Gen Z individuals might engage in behaviors that can be hurtful to others.

In the 90s, people didn't have the same level of online interaction, so interactions were often face-to-face or over the phone. This meant that communication was more personal, and people were more mindful of each other's feelings.

Today, with social media, it's easier to say things without considering how they might affect someone else. People might post hurtful comments or messages without realizing the impact they can have on others.

It's important for Gen Z to be aware of the impact of their words and actions, both online and offline. By practicing empathy and kindness, they can help create a more positive culture where people treat each other with respect and understanding.

> "*kindness is a timeless value that transcends generations. Whether it's Generation Z, Generation X, or any other generation, acts of kindness are universally appreciated and valued and they'll always be .*"

Kindness is a fundamental aspect of human nature that is cherished across cultures and throughout history. Regardless of age or background, people recognize the importance of kindness in fostering positive relationships, building communities, and creating a more compassionate world.

In every generation, there are individuals who exemplify kindness through their actions, words, and attitudes. They inspire others to follow their example and demonstrate the enduring power of kindness to make a difference in people's lives.

While societal trends and technological advancements may influence how kindness is expressed or perceived in different generations, the core essence of kindness remains unchanged. It is a fundamental human virtue that is celebrated and cherished by people of all ages, and its importance will continue to be recognized by future generations.

I believe in the power of kindness as a fundamental principle in both writing and life. It's essential to approach storytelling and interactions with empathy, understanding, and a genuine desire to uplift others.

In my writing, I strive to weave narratives that highlight the beauty of human connection, the importance of compassion, and the transformative impact of acts of kindness. Through my characters and their journeys, I aim to showcase the depth of human emotions, the complexities of relationships, and the significance of empathy in navigating life's challenges.

Moreover, I recognize the importance of self-care and setting healthy boundaries as an author. While storytelling is a deeply rewarding endeavor, it's also essential to prioritize my own well-being and ensure that I don't compromise my mental, emotional, or physical health in the process.

In both my writing and personal interactions, I endeavor to foster a culture of kindness, where empathy, respect, and understanding are at the forefront. By promoting compassion and empathy in my work and daily life, I hope to contribute to a more inclusive, supportive, and empathetic world where kindness flourishes.

Growing up alongside my grandparents, I've been fortunate to witness firsthand the enduring power of kindness woven into the fabric of everyday life. Their gentle words, compassionate actions, and unwavering support have left an indelible mark on my heart, shaping the person I am today.

From a young age, my grandparents instilled in me the values of empathy, generosity, and compassion through their simple yet profound acts of kindness. Whether it was offering a listening ear, lending a helping hand to those in need, or sharing stories of resilience and love, they taught me the importance of reaching out to others with open arms and an open heart.

Being in the presence of my grandparents, I learned that kindness is not merely a fleeting gesture but a way of life—a guiding principle that infuses joy, warmth, and meaning into every interaction. Their unwavering kindness towards others, regardless of background or circumstance, inspired me to embrace empathy and understanding as guiding forces in my own journey.

Moreover, my grandparents exemplified the transformative power of kindness in fostering deep connections and nurturing relationships. Their genuine care and concern for others created a ripple effect of positivity and goodwill, leaving a lasting impact on everyone they encountered.

As I navigate through life, the lessons of kindness imparted by my grandparents serve as a compass, guiding me towards acts of compassion, empathy, and generosity. Their legacy of kindness continues to inspire me to cherish the beauty of human connection, to extend a helping hand to those in need, and to embrace the transformative power of empathy in fostering a more inclusive and compassionate world.

In essence, my journey with my grandparents has instilled within me a profound appreciation for the enduring significance of kindness—a timeless value that I will cherish and carry with me all through my life.

Certainly! Kindness is a fundamental aspect of human interaction that holds immense power to shape our relationships, communities, and the world at large. When we choose kindness, we not only uplift others but also foster a culture of empathy, compassion, and understanding.

One of the remarkable aspects of kindness is its simplicity. It doesn't require grand gestures or elaborate displays. Kindness can manifest in the smallest acts, such as offering a smile to a stranger, lending a listening ear to a friend in need, or expressing gratitude to someone who has helped us. These seemingly insignificant gestures have the potential to brighten someone's day, ease their burdens, and create a ripple effect of positivity.

Moreover, kindness is contagious. When we extend kindness to others, it often inspires them to pay it forward, creating a chain reaction of goodwill. In this way, a single act of kindness can have far-reaching consequences, spreading joy and fostering a sense of interconnectedness among people.

Beyond its immediate effects on individuals, kindness also contributes to building strong, resilient communities. When people feel valued, respected, and supported, they are more likely to work together toward common goals, overcome challenges, and create positive change. In environments where kindness thrives, trust and cooperation flourish, leading to greater harmony and social cohesion.

Furthermore, kindness has the power to transform our own lives. When we approach interactions with an attitude of kindness and empathy, we cultivate a sense of inner peace, fulfillment, and purpose. Research has shown that acts of kindness not only benefit the recipient but also have positive effects on the giver, such as reducing stress, boosting mood, and enhancing overall well-being.

In a world where negativity, division, and conflict often dominate the headlines, choosing kindness becomes all the more important. By embodying kindness in our words and actions, we can counteract negativity, bridge divides, and build bridges of understanding. Kindness serves as a beacon of hope, reminding us of our shared humanity and the potential for positive change.

> *"Indeed, the saying "being human and human being makes a lot of difference" encapsulates a profound truth about the essence of humanity. While both terms refer to our species, they imply distinct qualities and behaviors that define our interactions with others and our approach to life."*

To be human is to possess the biological characteristics and attributes that distinguish us from other animals. It encompasses our physical form, cognitive abilities, and evolutionary heritage. However, being human goes beyond mere existence; it implies a deeper understanding of our shared humanity and a recognition of our interconnectedness with all living beings.

On the other hand, being a human being implies a set of moral and ethical principles that guide our actions and interactions with others. It encompasses qualities such as empathy, compassion, integrity, and respect for the dignity and rights of every individual. Being a human being involves embracing our capacity for kindness, understanding, and altruism, and striving to live in harmony with others and the world around us.

The distinction between being human and being a human being lies in how we choose to embody our humanity. While being human is an inherent trait, being a human being is a conscious choice—a commitment to live with integrity, empathy, and compassion. It's about recognizing that our actions have consequences and striving to make a positive impact on the lives of others.

In essence, being human is a biological reality, but being a human being is a moral and ethical imperative. It's about transcending our individual concerns and recognizing our responsibility to contribute to the well-being of others and the greater good. By embracing our humanity and striving to be true human beings, we can create a more compassionate, just, and harmonious world for all.

VI

RELEASE EXPECTATIONS, EMBRACE MIRACLES

"*Allowing the Universe to Work Its Magic.*"

The moment we release our expectations of others marks a profound shift in our perception and experience of life. Expectations often carry with them a weight of anticipation and attachment, which can lead to disappointment and frustration when they are not met. However, when we relinquish these expectations and free ourselves from the burden of anticipation, we open the door to a deeper sense of peace, contentment, and liberation.

Expectations are often rooted in our desires, beliefs, and past experiences, shaping the way we interact with others and perceive the world around us. We may expect certain behaviors, actions, or outcomes from those around us based on our own needs and assumptions. However, when these expectations are not met, it can lead to feelings of resentment, hurt, or disillusionment.

The truth is, no one owes us anything, and expecting others to fulfill our needs or meet our expectations only sets us up for disappointment. Each person is on their own journey, with their own challenges, limitations, and priorities. When we release our expectations of others, we free ourselves from the need for validation or approval and allow them to be who they are, without judgment or pressure.

Moreover, releasing expectations opens up space for authentic connections and meaningful relationships to flourish. When we approach others with an open heart and mind, free from preconceived notions or demands, we create an environment of acceptance, understanding, and mutual respect. We can appreciate people for who they are, rather than who we want them to be, and cultivate deeper, more fulfilling connections based on genuine care and affection.

Ultimately, the day we stop expecting from others is the day we reclaim our power and take responsibility for our own happiness and well-being. It is a liberating moment of self-realization, where we recognize that our peace of mind and fulfillment are not dependent on external circumstances or other people's actions. Instead, they arise from within us, from our ability to accept life as it is and find contentment in the present moment.

So, let us release our expectations of others and embrace the freedom and joy that come with living authentically and without attachment. Let us trust in the wisdom of life's unfolding journey and allow ourselves to be guided by the flow of grace and possibility. In doing so, we may discover that the greatest gift we can give ourselves is the gift of letting go.

"Release Expectations, Embrace Miracles" serves as a powerful reminder of the transformative power that comes with letting go and surrendering to the flow of life. In a world where we are often taught to set goals, plan meticulously, and strive tirelessly towards specific outcomes, the concept of releasing expectations may initially seem counterintuitive. However, upon closer examination, it becomes evident that this approach holds the key to unlocking a deeper sense of peace, fulfillment, and joy in our lives.

At its core, "Release Expectations, Embrace Miracles" is about relinquishing attachment to specific outcomes and trusting in the natural ebb and flow of life. It is a recognition that holding onto rigid expectations only serves to limit our potential and create unnecessary stress and anxiety. Instead of constantly trying to control every aspect of our lives, we are encouraged to surrender to the wisdom of the universe and allow things to unfold organically.

One of the fundamental principles underlying this concept is the understanding that attachment to outcomes often stems from a place of fear or insecurity. We may cling tightly to certain expectations because we believe that they hold the key to our happiness or success. However, in doing so, we inadvertently block the flow of abundance and opportunities that are trying to make their way into our lives. By releasing these expectations and embracing a mindset of trust and surrender, we create space for miracles to occur.

Letting go of expectations does not mean abandoning our goals or aspirations. Rather, it is a shift in perspective—a willingness to detach from the outcome and focus instead on the present moment. When we release the need to control every aspect of our lives, we allow ourselves to be guided by intuition and inspiration, opening the door to new possibilities and pathways that we may not have previously considered.

Embracing miracles requires a willingness to see beyond the limitations of our rational minds and tap into the infinite potential that lies within each of us. It is a recognition that the universe is abundant and infinitely creative, and that miracles are constantly unfolding all around us if we are willing to open our hearts and minds to receive them. Whether it's a chance encounter, a serendipitous opportunity, or a sudden breakthrough, miracles come in many forms, and when we release our expectations, we create space for them to manifest in our lives.

Practicing the art of releasing expectations and embracing miracles is not always easy. It requires a willingness to let go of the need for certainty and control, and to surrender to the unknown with faith and trust. However, the rewards of this practice are profound. As we learn to release our grip on specific outcomes and trust in the wisdom of the universe, we discover a newfound sense of freedom, joy, and abundance that transcends our wildest dreams.

In conclusion, "Release Expectations, Embrace Miracles" invites us to loosen our grip on the steering wheel of life and surrender to the flow of the river. It is a reminder that when we let go of expectations and open ourselves up to the infinite possibilities that exist in every moment, we invite miracles to unfold in our lives in ways that are beyond our wildest imagination. So let us release our expectations, embrace the unknown, and allow the magic of life to unfold in all its splendor.

> *"A key idea from "The Secret" by Rhonda Byrne is that if you really, really want something and you ask the universe for it with all your heart, the universe will help you make it happen. It's like when you wish for something really strongly, it's like sending out a message to the universe. And according to the book, when you do that, the universe sends back things that match what you asked for. So, it's saying that if you focus on what you want and believe it will happen, it's more likely to come true. It's all about thinking positively and believing in your dreams."*

VII

Do SONGS TEACH US MORE THAN WE REALIZE ?

"From Melody to Meaning"

As a kid who loved music, I've always enjoyed singing along to songs and listening to different kinds of music. When I was 14, I discovered Tamil folk songs and was fascinated by their lively beats and meaningful lyrics. Even when I was 12 or 13, I fell in love with the old Bollywood songs from the early 20s. They had a special charm that made me feel nostalgic and transported me to a different time.

As I got older, I started exploring modern songs too. I loved the catchy tunes and emotional lyrics that spoke to me in different ways. Music has always been more than just something to listen to for me. It's been a source of happiness, comfort, and inspiration.

No matter what's going on in my life, music has always been there for me. It's like a friend that I can always count on to lift my spirits and make me feel better. Whether I'm singing along to my favorite songs or just listening to them, music has a way of making everything seem better.

I'm really grateful for the impact that music has had on my life. It's taught me so much and given me so many wonderful memories. I know that no matter where life takes me, music will always be there to help me through.

Looking up at the stars with my earpods in is one of my favorite things to do. It's a peaceful time when I can escape from the noise of the world and just enjoy the beauty of the night sky. I pick out my favorite songs to listen to and press play, letting the music fill my ears.

As I listen, I tilt my head back and watch the stars twinkling above. They seem to dance along with the music, making the whole experience feel magical. The songs I'm listening to suddenly feel more meaningful, like they're telling stories that I can relate to.

It's like the stars are joining in with the music, adding their own special touch to the songs. They shine brightly in the dark sky, making everything feel calm and peaceful. In those moments, I feel like I'm a part of something bigger than myself, connected to the universe in a special way.

When the music finally fades away, I take out my earpods and go back to the real world. But I always hold onto the memory of that special time when I was able to relax and enjoy the beauty of the stars while listening to my favorite songs. It's a simple pleasure, but it brings me so much joy and peace.

I'm excited to share some special song lyrics that mean a lot to me. These lyrics have been like little lights in the dark, giving me hope and comfort when things get tough.

They're more than just words; they're like friends that help me through hard times.

The Bollywood movie "Rockstar" stands out not only as one of the most inspiring films I've had the pleasure of watching but also as one of the biggest successes in the realm of Indian cinema. From its captivating storyline to its mesmerizing performances, "Rockstar" has left an indelible mark on audiences worldwide, resonating deeply with viewers of all ages and backgrounds.

"Rockstar" is more than just a movie—it's an experience, a journey that resonates on a profound level with anyone who has ever dared to dream. Its universal themes, compelling performances, and unforgettable music have made it a timeless classic, inspiring audiences to pursue their passions and embrace life's challenges with courage and conviction. For me, "Rockstar" will always hold a special place in my heart, serving as a constant reminder of the power of dreams and the beauty of following one's heart.

What makes "Rockstar" really special is its amazing music by A.R. Rahman. The songs in the movie are so powerful—they can make you feel all kinds of emotions. Whether it's a slow, heartfelt song or a fast-paced rock anthem, the music stays with you long after the movie ends. It's like a journey for your soul, touching your heart in so many ways.

1.***"Nadaan parinde"***

"Kaaga re kaaga re mori itni araj tose
Chun chun khaaiyo maans
Kaaga re kaaga re mori itni araj tose
Chun chun khaaiyo maans

Arajiya re khaaiyo na tu naina more
Khaaiyon na tu naina mohe
Piya ke milan ki aas
Khaaiyon na tu naina more
Khaaiyon na tu naina mohe
Piya ke milan ki aas
"

i love the way these lines said O crow, I have so much of request to you, eat (my body's) flesh,
but do not eat my eyes, don't eat my eyes as I have a wish to see my lover.:

Matter of fact, this part of the song is almost completely different from the rest of the world, but at the same time is important here as it tells where the singer thinks his home is.

From my understanding, "Kaaga" in the context of the song does indeed refer to a crow, not any other bird. The term "Kaaga" originates from the Sanskrit word "Kaak," which is commonly used to describe a crow in various dialects, including Awadhi and Braj. Therefore, it's clear that the singer is referring to a crow.

Furthermore, the symbolism of the crow in mythology and science adds depth to its portrayal in the song. Crows are often associated with scavenging and feeding on carrion, which aligns with the singer's reference to the crow eating flesh.

Additionally, the mention of the "naadaan parinda" or immature bird serves as a metaphor for the singer themselves. They describe themselves as someone who has lost their home and is navigating through the unknown paths of life alone. This metaphorical interpretation separates the crow from the naive bird mentioned in the song, emphasizing that they are two distinct entities.

Overall, the use of "Kaaga" in the song carries symbolic significance, portraying the crow as a scavenger and highlighting the singer's own struggles and journey through life.

2."Kun Faya Kun"

> *“"Ho mujhpe karam sarkar tera Araj tujhe kar de mujhe Mujhse hi riha Ab mujhko bhi ho deedar mera Kar de mujhe mujhse hi riha, mujhse hi riha"”*

These lines express a longing for divine grace and guidance. The singer implores their master (sarkar) for mercy (karam) and liberation (riha) from their worldly burdens. They yearn to experience the presence (deedar) of their beloved, seeking release from their inner turmoil and a connection to something greater.

> *“"Mann ke mere yeh bharam Kachche mere yeh karam Leke chale hain kahaan Main to jaanu hi na"”*

Here, the singer reflects on their doubts (bharam) and flawed actions (kachche karam) that have led them astray.

They ponder their direction in life (kahaan leke chale hain) and express uncertainty (main to jaanu hi na) about their path forward.

> *“"Tu hai mujh mein samaaya kahaan leke mujhe aaya Main hoon tujh mein samaaya tere peeche chala aaya Tera hi main ik saaya tune mujhko banaya Main toh jag ko naa bhaaya Tune gale se lagaya haan phir tu hi hai khudaya Sacch tu hi hai khudaya aa"”*

These lines speak to the singer’s realization of divine presence within themselves (tu hai mujh mein samaaya) and their journey towards self-discovery and spiritual awakening. They acknowledge being guided by a higher power (tu hi hai khudaya) and express gratitude for being embraced (tune gale se lagaya) by the divine.

Overall, the song "Kun Faya Kun" encapsulates the essence of the spiritual themes explored in my book, serving as a guiding light for readers on their own quest for inner liberation and divine connection.

3. phir se udd chala

> *“Mitti jaise sapne ye kitna bhi palko se jhaado*
> *Phir aa jaate hain*
> *Itne saare sapne kya kahoon*
> *Kis tarah se maine tode hain, chhode hain, kyun*
> *Mere saath chale, mujhe le ke ude, ye kyun”*

"Mitti jaise sapne ye kitna bhi palko se jhaado, Phir aa jaate hain": This line talks about how dreams are like dust. Even if you try to forget about them by closing your eyes (like brushing them away with your eyelids), they still come back. It shows that dreams are strong and keep coming back, even if you try to ignore them. It's like when you have a dream that keeps coming back to your mind, no matter what you do.

"Itne saare sapne kya kahoon, Kis tarah se maine tode hain, chhode hain, kyun":This line talks about thinking about all the dreams the singer has had. They're wondering how they've let go of some of these dreams. They're thinking about why they gave up on these dreams and reflecting on the choices they've made. It shows how it's hard to chase dreams because of the challenges we face in life.

"Mere saath chale, mujhe le ke ude, ye kyun""In this last line, the singer asks why dreams stick with them and keep lifting them up. They're wondering about the reason these dreams stay with them and give them hope on their journey through life. It shows how dreams have a big impact on making people want to reach their goals and imagine a better future. It's like they're amazed by how dreams can give them strength and help them through tough times.

4."Teri Deewani" by Kailash Kher

> "*Ishq junoon jab hadh se badh jaaye*
> *Haste haste aashiq sooli chadh jaaye*
> *Ishq ka jaadu sar chadhkar bole*
> *Khoob laga lo pehre raste rab khole*
> *Yahi ishq di marzi hai, yahi rab di marzi hai*"

"Ishq Junoon" convey profound lessons that i can really resonate to .

"When the love for something crosses boundaries" teaches me about the power of passion and dedication. It reminds me that when I truly care about something, whether it's a goal, a relationship, or a dream, I am willing to go above and beyond to achieve it.

"Haste haste aashiq sooli chadh jaaye" reminds me of the resilience and determination required to overcome obstacles. It teaches me to face challenges with a positive attitude and to persevere, even in the face of adversity.

"Ishq ka jaadu sar chadhkar bole" inspires me to embrace the transformative power of love. It reminds me that love has the ability to uplift and inspire, filling my life with joy and meaning.

"Khoob laga lo pehre raste rab khole" reminds me to trust in the journey of life. It teaches me to have faith that when I put my heart and soul into my endeavors, the universe will conspire to guide me towards my destiny.

And finally, "Yahi ishq di marzi hai, yahi rab di marzi hai" reminds me to surrender to the will of love and fate. It teaches me to accept that some things are beyond my control and to trust in the divine plan that unfolds before me.

Overall, these lyrics have taught me valuable lessons about passion, resilience, faith, and surrender. They serve as a constant source of inspiration and guidance in my journey through life.

5. "jiya re "

"Halke halke pardo mein
Muskurana achha lagta hai
Roshni jo deta ho toh
Dil jalana achha lagta hai
Ek pal sahi, umr bhar isey sath rakhna Akira
Zindagi se phir ek waada maine kar liya re
Jiya jiya re jiya re"

The lyrics from Gulzar's song *"Jiya Jiya Re Jiya Re"* convey a deep sense of contentment and fulfillment in life's simple joys and experiences.

"Halke Halke, Pardon Mein, Muskurana Achcha Lagta Hai" celebrates the beauty of smiling softly, even behind the veil of modesty. It suggests that finding joy in the little moments and sharing a gentle smile can bring a sense of warmth and happiness.

"Roshni Jo Deta Ho To, Dil Jalana Achcha Lagta Hai" expresses the idea that experiencing the brightness and warmth of light can be comforting, even if it means enduring the burning sensation of the heart. It portrays the paradoxical nature of finding solace in both light and warmth, despite the pain it may bring.

"Ek Pal Sahi, Umr Bhar Use, Saath Rakhta Akira" reflects on the significance of cherishing fleeting moments of happiness and carrying their memory throughout one's lifetime. It emphasizes the enduring impact of brief moments of joy, which can stay with us forever.

"Zindagi Se Phir Ek Vaada Maine Kar Liya Re" signifies a personal commitment to life and its experiences. It suggests making a promise to embrace life fully, with all its ups and downs, and to cherish each moment, no matter how brief.

These words from Gulzar show how he understands life really well. He talks about how it's important to be happy with simple things, enjoy the little moments, and keep the promises we make to ourselves.

In my life, there's something I do that's kind of unusual. I like to connect songs with people I care about, like friends or family. It's a nice way to show them how much they mean to me. But sometimes, it can make me feel really sad.

See, when things are going well, sharing music with loved ones feels amazing. It's like we're sharing a special moment together. But if something goes wrong in our relationship, the same songs that used to make me happy can suddenly make me feel really down.

It's like those songs become reminders of the good times we had, and it hurts to think about them now that things aren't so great. It's a bit of a bummer, honestly.

But even though it can be tough, I try to remember that feeling things deeply is just part of being human. And I know that even though some songs might make me sad now, they've also brought me a lot of joy in the past.

So, I guess I'll keep listening to those songs, even if they make me feel a little sad sometimes. Because in the end, they're still a part of my story, and that's pretty special.

If only I could share every song from my cherished playlist with you right here and now! Alas, the constraints of this moment prevent such a feat. However, the desire remains strong within me to someday compile these beloved melodies into a separate book, a tribute to the rhythms and harmonies that have woven themselves into the fabric of my life.

In the depths of my playlist lie countless stories waiting to be told, each song a chapter in the unfolding narrative of my existence. From the nostalgic melodies of yesteryear to the pulsating beats of modern tunes, each track holds a special place in my heart, evoking memories, emotions, and dreams.

In this envisioned book, I would delve into the significance of each song, sharing personal anecdotes, reflections, and insights into how they have shaped my journey. It would be a labor of love, a testament to the power of music to uplift, inspire, and transcend the boundaries of time and space.

Until the day comes when this dream becomes a reality, I hold onto the melodies in my heart, cherishing each note and lyric as a treasured piece of my soul's soundtrack. And when the time is right, I'll share the stories behind these songs with the world, inviting others to join me on a musical journey through the tapestry of life.

To anyone reading this book, even if we haven't kept in touch, I want you to know something important: I still listen to our songs, and I cherish them just as much as ever. Even if time has passed and things may have changed between us, the memories we shared through those songs are still close to my heart. So, if you ever find yourself flipping through these pages, remember that our connection lives on in the music we once loved together.

VIII

THE JOURNEY CONTINUES

"Kehte hain agar kisi cheez ko dil se chaho ... to puri kainaat usse tumse milane ki koshish mein lag jaati hai..."

Many of you may recognize this iconic dialogue from the movie OM SHANTI OM. Whenever I utter these words, my hand automatically strikes a Shahrukh Khan pose. It might seem funny, but I never imagined that one day I would take this dialogue seriously enough to include it in my very first book.

It's kind of like when you wish for something so hard, and suddenly, it's like the universe is listening and everything starts falling into place. It's happened to me before, and it's pretty amazing.

This idea teaches us to believe in our dreams and to keep thinking positive thoughts. It's all about aiming for what we really want and trusting that good things will come our way if we believe in them strongly enough.

So, let's remember Shah Rukh Khan's words and never stop dreaming big. Who knows? Maybe the universe is listening, and our wishes are closer than we think.

> "*maybe that's how manifestation works!!!*"

In the quiet moments of introspection, I find myself drawn to the stars, their twinkling lights a source of comfort and inspiration. "While Staring at the Stars" encapsulates not just a mere activity but a profound metaphor for my inner journey—a journey of self-exploration, growth, and ultimately, finding my place in the universe.

I realize that my obsession lies not only in gazing at the stars above but also in the act of writing from within. It's a journey inward, a process of unraveling the complexities of my thoughts, emotions, and experiences.

Writing from within has become my sanctuary, a sacred space where I can unravel the complexities of my thoughts and emotions. Each word, each sentence, is a brushstroke on the canvas of my soul, painting a picture of my hopes, dreams, and aspirations.

> "*As I pen down these words, I acknowledge that I am a lost girl, adrift in the vastness of existence, yearning for someone to offer a guiding hand and illuminate the path ahead. Yet, amidst the uncertainty, there exists a glimmer of hope—a belief*

> *that somewhere out there, someone sees the beauty in my brokenness, the light in my darkness."*

The journey continues, not as a linear progression but as a winding path filled with twists and turns, challenges and triumphs. It is a journey of self-discovery, of learning to embrace my flaws and imperfections, and finding strength in vulnerability.

> *"Yet, as I embark on this journey, I am keenly aware that it is only the beginning. Life is a continuous evolution, a series of chapters waiting to be written. While I may be a lost girl at this moment, I hold onto the belief that someday, someone will come along to rescue me—to shine a light in the darkness and guide me towards a brighter future."*

> *"With each step forward, I am reminded to be grateful—for the love that surrounds me, the lessons that shape me, and the moments that take my breath away. For even in the darkest of nights, the stars shine brightly, offering guidance and reassurance that I am not alone."*

In the quiet moments of reflection, I often find myself marveling at the intricacies of life, pondering the paths I've traveled and the ones that lie ahead. Each step forward is a testament to resilience, to the strength found in embracing the unknown with unwavering faith.

With each passing day, I am reminded of the countless blessings that have graced my journey—the laughter shared with loved ones, the tears shed in moments of vulnerability, the triumphs and failures that have shaped me into who I am today. Each experience, whether joyous or challenging, has left an indelible mark on my soul, weaving together the tapestry of my existence.

As I gaze up at the stars, their twinkling lights a beacon of hope in the darkness, I am filled with a profound sense of gratitude. Gratitude for the opportunities that have come my way, for the lessons learned, and for the people who have touched my life in ways both big and small.

But amidst the gratitude, there is also a sense of anticipation—a stirring within my heart that whispers of adventures yet to unfold, of dreams waiting to be realized. It is this sense of possibility that propels me forward, urging me to embrace each new day with courage and optimism.

> "*For while I may be a lost girl in this vast universe, I am also a seeker—a seeker of truth, of meaning, of connection. And though the journey ahead may be filled with twists and turns, I trust in the wisdom of the stars to guide me on my path.*"

So I continue to stare at the stars, not just with fascination, but with a deep sense of gratitude for the journey that lies ahead. For in the midst of uncertainty, there is beauty to be found, and in the embrace of the unknown, there is freedom to discover the true depths of my being.

And so, with an open heart and a spirit of adventure, I step boldly into the future, knowing that the best is yet to come. For the journey continues, and with each passing moment, I am reminded of the infinite possibilities that await me in the vast expanse of the universe.

So I will continue to stare at the stars, with wonder and awe, knowing that within their infinite expanse lies the promise of endless possibilities. And as the journey

unfolds, I will embrace it wholeheartedly, for it is through the journey that I discover who I truly am and what I am capable of becoming.

Certainly! Here's a longer version of the passage:

> ***"As I contemplate the trajectory of my life and ponder the uncertain road that lies ahead, the words of the renowned poet Robert Frost echo in my mind: "Two roads diverged in a wood, and I—I took the one less traveled by." These simple yet profound words resonate deeply within me, encapsulating my resolve to embark on a journey marked by uniqueness, adventure, and self-discovery."***

In a world where conformity often reigns supreme, I have chosen to deviate from the beaten path, opting instead for the road less traveled. This decision is not born out of a desire for rebellion or defiance, but rather stems from a yearning for authenticity and individuality. I am drawn to the allure of the unknown, to the untamed wilderness of possibility that awaits me beyond the confines of convention.

Admittedly, the road less traveled is not without its challenges. It is rife with obstacles, uncertainties, and unexpected twists and turns. Yet, it is precisely these challenges that imbue the journey with meaning and significance. Each obstacle overcome, each setback endured, serves as a testament to my resilience and fortitude, strengthening my resolve to press onward.

While I cannot predict with certainty what the future holds, I embrace the uncertainty with open arms. I see it not as a hindrance, but as an opportunity—a blank canvas upon which I can paint the tapestry of my own destiny. I am unafraid of the unknown, for I trust in my ability to navigate its uncharted waters with courage and conviction.

The road less traveled is not just a physical path; it is a metaphor for life itself—a symbol of the choices we make and the journeys we undertake. It is a reminder that true fulfillment lies not in following the crowd, but in charting our own course, guided by our passions, values, and aspirations.

As I traverse this less traveled road, I am filled with a sense of anticipation and excitement. Each step forward is a step into the unknown, a leap of faith into the vast expanse of possibility. I am eager to explore the uncharted territories that lie ahead, to discover new landscapes, forge new connections, and uncover hidden truths.

But amidst the uncertainty, there is also a profound sense of gratitude—for the opportunities that have shaped me, for the experiences that have molded me, and for the people who have supported me along the way. I am grateful for the freedom to choose my own path, to carve out my own destiny in a world brimming with endless possibilities.

In the end, it is not the destination that matters most, but the journey itself. And so, I embrace the road less traveled with open arms, knowing that it is on this path that I will find fulfillment, purpose, and true self-discovery.

Above all, I hold onto the belief that kindness is a reflection of something greater than ourselves. It is a manifestation of the divine love that flows through each and every one of us, a reminder of the goodness that exists in the world, even in the midst of hardship and strife. And so, as I journey forward, I hold fast to my commitment to kindness, knowing that it is not just a wish, but a way of life—a way of honoring the divine presence that guides and sustains us all.

At the end of the day, my biggest wish is to always be kind to others. I truly believe that kindness is key to making the world a better place. And above all, I have faith in God, knowing that He is watching over me and guiding me along the way.

I Am Indebted To You For...

As I write these words, I realize that I feel both lost and hopeful at the same time. It's like I'm wandering without a clear direction, unsure of where I'm headed. But deep down, I still hold onto my dreams. Even though I'm not sure what the future holds, I'm determined to keep dreaming and believing in better days ahead.

I want to extend my deepest gratitude to all of you who have joined me on this journey by reading my book. Your support, encouragement, and companionship throughout this experience have been invaluable to me. Whether you've been with me from the very beginning, eagerly turning the pages as the story unfolded, or whether you discovered my book along the way and decided to join in, your presence has made a profound impact. Your willingness to embark on this adventure with me, to immerse yourselves in the world I've created, and to share in the joys and challenges depicted within its pages, means more to me than words can express.

Each reader who has picked up my book has become a fellow traveler on this literary voyage, and for that, I am deeply grateful. Your interest in my story, your engagement with its themes and characters, and your willingness to invest your time and attention have filled me with immense appreciation and humility. It is your curiosity, your enthusiasm, and your support that have fueled my passion for writing and inspired me to continue sharing my voice with the world.

As I reflect on this journey we've taken together, I am filled with a sense of awe and gratitude for the connections we've forged, the insights we've gained, and the memories we've created along the way. Your presence has transformed this solitary pursuit of writing into a shared experience, a communal celebration of storytelling and imagination. Whether you've laughed, cried, or been moved by the words on these pages, please know that your presence has made a difference in my life, and for that, I am profoundly thankful.

So, from the bottom of my heart, thank you for reading my book and for being with me through every twist and turn of this adventure. Your support has been a beacon of light, guiding me through the challenges and illuminating the path forward.

That young girl, who once harbored the dream of writing a book, must now be overwhelmed with a whirlwind of emotions as she sees her aspiration and dreams materialize before her eyes. The sense of accomplishment she feels is likely palpable, a result of the hard work, dedication, and perseverance she poured into bringing her vision to life. There's undoubtedly a profound sense of fulfillment coursing through her veins, knowing that she has transformed her once-distant dream into a tangible reality.

She must feel an overwhelming sense of pride and accomplishment as she holds her book in her hands, a tangible symbol of her hard work and dedication. The journey from aspiring writer to published author must feel like a surreal dream come true, filled with moments of doubt and uncertainty overcome by sheer determination. She must marvel at how each word she penned has culminated in this beautiful creation, a testament to her creativity and passion.

As she flips through the pages, she must feel a rush of emotions—joy, excitement, perhaps a hint of nervousness—as she prepares to share her story with the world. She must reflect on the countless hours spent honing her craft, the late nights and early mornings sacrificed in pursuit of her dreams. And amidst the pride and satisfaction, she must feel a profound sense of gratitude for the opportunity to share her voice and her vision with others.

Looking back on her journey, she must feel a sense of awe at how far she's come. From the initial spark of inspiration to the final flourish of her pen, every step of the writing process has shaped her into the person she is today. She must recognize the growth and transformation that has occurred along the way, both as a writer and as an individual.

Now, as she prepares to embark on this new chapter of her life as a published author, she must feel a mix of excitement and apprehension for the road ahead. She must wonder how her book will be received by readers, hoping that her words will resonate with and inspire others. But above all, she must feel a deep sense of fulfillment, knowing that she had the courage to pursue her dreams and see them through to fruition.

In the end, she must stand as a shining example of what is possible when passion meets perseverance. She must serve as a reminder that no dream is too big, no goal too daunting, as long as one is willing to believe in themselves and chase after their dreams with unwavering determination. And as she looks towards the future, she must do so with a heart full of hope and a sense of boundless possibility.

> *"As we part ways at the conclusion of this book, please know that your impact on me and my writing journey will endure long after the final page has been turned."*

www.ingramcontent.com/pod-product-compliance
Lightning Source LLC
La Vergne TN
LVHW041235150826
845673LV00008B/2385

9798893224580